EVERYTHING SPORTS ALMANACS

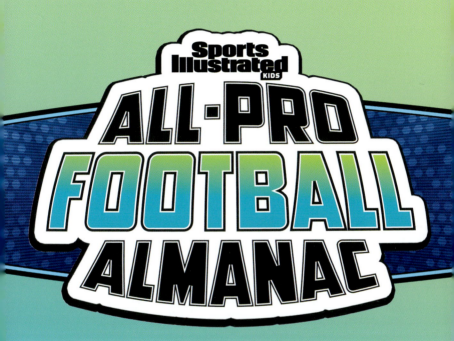

BY PATRICK DONNELLY

CAPSTONE PRESS
a capstone imprint

Published by Capstone Press, an imprint of Capstone
1710 Roe Crest Drive, North Mankato, Minnesota 56003
capstonepub.com

Copyright © 2026 by Capstone. All rights reserved. No part of this publication may be reproduced in whole or in part, or stored in a retrieval system, or transmitted in any form or by any means, electronic, mechanical, photocopying, recording, or otherwise, without written permission of the publisher.

SPORTS ILLUSTRATED KIDS is a trademark of ABG-SI LLC. Used with permission.

Library of Congress Cataloging-in-Publication Data is available on the Library of Congress website.

ISBN: 9798875232749 (hardcover)
ISBN: 9798875232695 (paperback)
ISBN: 9798875232701 (ebook PDF)

Summary: Exciting pro football facts in a variety of formats keep excited sports fans turning the pages.

Editorial Credits
Editor: Mandy Robbins; Designer: Sarah Bennett; Media Researcher: Rebekah Hubstenberger; Production Specialist: Tori Abraham

Image Credits
Associated Press; 4, Harry Cabluck, 18, Paul Spinelli/NFL Photos, 42, Ron Riesterer, 44; Getty Images: Al Bello, 33 (top right), Andy Lyons, 40 (top right), Chris Graythen, cover (top), 17, Earl Richardson/Allsport, 46, George Rose, 11 (top), Hannah Foslien, cover (bottom right), 22, Harry How, 28, Jamie Squire, cover (bottom left), 12, Joe Robbins, 47, Joe Sargent, 37, Julio Aguilar, 34 (middle right), Katelyn Mulcahy, 29, Kevin C. Cox, 33 (middle left), Michael Hickey, 41, Michael Reaves, 27, Patrick Smith, 5, Robert Gauthier/Los Angeles Times, 30, Ron Jenkins, 34 (middle left), Scott Cunningham, 25, Stephen Maturen, 40 (top left), Tom Hauck/Allsport, 38, William Purnell/Icon Sportswire, 15 (top); Shutterstock: adam_wasikowski, 10 (map), Andrew Angelov, 15 (middle), Brocreative, 39 (background), Design_Lands, 39 (footballs), E2.art.lab, 8 (middle), EFKS, 4-5 (background), Fallen Knight (holographic background), cover and throughout, grey_and (football), back cover and throughout, LIORIKI, 13, 23, 31, 43, mentalmind, 5 (gold stars), MyPro, 19, Olga Moonlight, 6-7 (background), RNko7, 3 (background), Ronnie Chua, 45 (background), StarLine, back cover (background), Steve Collender, 8 (top left), The Blue Portrait, 8 (arrow), Uglegorets, 45 (football field top view), Vlad Ra27 (NFL logo and NFL team logos), 6-7, 10, Yauheni Meshcharakou, 21, zieusin, 16; Sports Illustrated: David E. Klutho, 35, Erick W. Rasco, 9, John Iacono, 36, John W. McDonough, 32, Neil Leifer, 26, Peter Read Miller, 20-21, Simon Bruty, 24

Any additional websites and resources referenced in this book are not maintained, authorized, or sponsored by Capstone. All product and company names are trademarks™ or registered® trademarks of their respective holders.

All stats are current through August 2025.

Table of Contents

About the League 4

Greatest Games 12

Standout Plays 18

Team Dynasties 24

Iconic Players 32

Record Breakers 40

About the League

» The Green Bay Packers face the New York Giants in 1938.

NFL HISTORY

The rough-and-tumble sport of football was invented in the late 1800s. It was popular at the college level for 50 years before the National Football League (NFL) was founded in 1920. Professional baseball had already taken the country by storm. Now it was football's turn.

Many teams came and went in the early years. By the mid-1930s, the league began to look more like it does today. The top teams included the Green Bay Packers, the Chicago Bears, and the New York Giants. The NFL was on its way to becoming the most popular league in the United States.

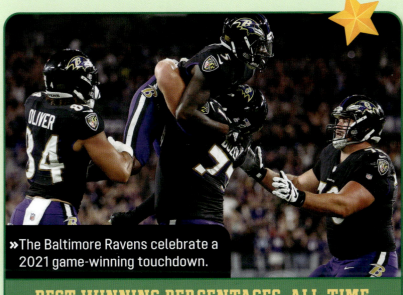

» The Baltimore Ravens celebrate a 2021 game-winning touchdown.

BEST WINNING PERCENTAGES, ALL-TIME

1. Dallas Cowboys (.576)
2. Green Bay Packers (.572)
3. Baltimore Ravens (.569)
4. Chicago Bears (.556)
5. New England Patriots (.555)

MEET THE TEAMS

NATIONAL FOOTBALL CONFERENCE (NFC)

Atlanta Falcons
Mercedes-Benz Stadium
Atlanta, GA

Minnesota Vikings
U.S. Bank Stadium
Minneapolis, MN

Arizona Cardinals
State Farm Stadium
Glendale, AZ

New Orleans Saints
Caesars Superdome
New Orleans, LA

Carolina Panthers
Bank of America Stadium
Charlotte, NC

New York Giants
MetLife Stadium
East Rutherford, NJ

Chicago Bears
Soldier Field
Chicago, IL

Philadelphia Eagles
Lincoln Financial Field
Philadelphia, PA

Dallas Cowboys
AT&T Stadium
Arlington, TX

San Francisco 49ers
Levi's Stadium
Santa Clara, CA

Detroit Lions
Ford Field
Detroit, MI

Seattle Seahawks
Lumen Field
Seattle, WA

Green Bay Packers
Lambeau Field
Green Bay, WI

Tampa Bay Buccaneers
Raymond James Stadium
Tampa, FL

Los Angeles Rams
SoFi Stadium
Inglewood, CA

Washington Commanders
Northwest Stadium
Landover, MD

AMERICAN FOOTBALL CONFERENCE (AFC)

Baltimore Ravens
M&T Bank Stadium
Baltimore, MD

Kansas City Chiefs
GEHA Field at Arrowhead Stadium
Kansas City, MO

Buffalo Bills
Highmark Stadium
Orchard Park, NY

Las Vegas Raiders
Allegiant Stadium
Las Vegas, NV

Cincinnati Bengals
Paycor Stadium
Cincinnati, OH

Los Angeles Chargers
SoFi Stadium
Inglewood, CA

Cleveland Browns
Huntington Bank Field
Cleveland, OH

Miami Dolphins
Hard Rock Stadium
Miami Gardens, FL

Denver Broncos
Empower Field at Mile High
Denver, CO

New England Patriots
Gillette Stadium
Foxborough, MA

Houston Texans
NRG Stadium
Houston, TX

New York Jets
MetLife Stadium
East Rutherford, NJ

Indianapolis Colts
Lucas Oil Stadium
Indianapolis, IN

Pittsburgh Steelers
Acrisure Stadium
Pittsburgh, PA

Jacksonville Jaguars
EverBank Stadium
Jacksonville, FL

Tennessee Titans
Nissan Stadium
Nashville, TN

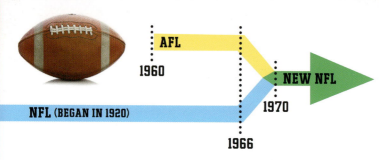

THE GREAT MERGER

The American Football League (AFL) began in 1960. It challenged the NFL. In 1966, the leagues agreed to merge. The AFL continued on its own through 1969. The first season of the "new" NFL was played in 1970.

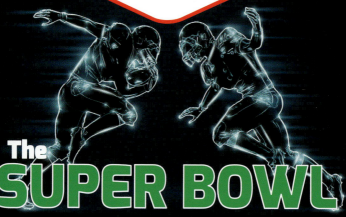

The SUPER BOWL

When the AFL and NFL agreed to merge, they didn't combine their schedules until 1970. Until then, each league continued to crown its own champion. But they agreed to one more game between the two champions. The first AFL-NFL World Championship Game was played on January 15, 1967.

The game was a big hit. By 1969, it had been renamed the Super Bowl. About 65 million people watched that first AFL-NFL World Championship Game on TV. In 2025, the Super Bowl drew about 127.7 million viewers.

MOST SUPER BOWL VICTORIES
New England Patriots, 6
Pittsburgh Steelers, 6
San Francisco 49ers, 5
Dallas Cowboys, 5
Green Bay Packers, 4
New York Giants, 4
Kansas City Chiefs, 4

» Philadelphia Eagles' Cooper DeJean celebrates with teammates after scoring a touchdown off of an interception during the 2024–2025 Super Bowl.

CARDINALS TAKE FLIGHT

The Cardinals are the oldest pro football team in the country. The team was formed in 1898. It has not always played in Arizona. A long and winding journey led them to the desert.

❶ Chicago – Founding members of the NFL, the Cardinals played here from 1920 to 1959.

❷ St. Louis – The Cardinals were tired of being viewed as a second-class team behind the Chicago Bears. The Cardinals moved 300 miles (480 km) to St. Louis, where they played from 1960 to 1987.

❸ Phoenix – After failing to secure funding for a new stadium, the Cardinals moved to Arizona. They were called the Phoenix Cardinals from 1988 to 1993 before changing to the Arizona Cardinals.

» The Phoenix Cardinals in action against Washington, 1988

MONDAY NIGHT FOOTBALL

Most NFL games are played on Sundays. In 1970, the NFL started playing games on Monday nights. Fans loved having a game to watch on a weeknight. Today, the league plays games regularly on Monday, Thursday, and Sunday.

Greatest Games

» James White celebrates his 1-yard touchdown.

PATRIOTS SHOCK FALCONS

On February 5, 2017, the New England Patriots faced the Atlanta Falcons in the Super Bowl. Atlanta led 28–3 late in the third quarter. Then the Patriots' Tom Brady threw two touchdown passes. Running back James White's 1-yard run and a two-point conversion tied the game 28–28.

For the first time, the Super Bowl went to overtime. New England got the ball and marched down the field. Another short touchdown run by White completed the comeback. The final score was Patriots 34, Falcons 28.

Biggest NFL Comebacks

December 17, 2022: **Vikings** trail Colts by 33, win 39–36

January 3, 1993: **Bills** trail Houston Oilers by 32, win 41–38 in overtime***

December 7, 1980: **49ers** trail Saints by 28, win 38–35

January 4, 2014: **Colts** trail Chiefs by 28, win 45–44***

January 14, 2023: **Jaguars** trail Chargers by 27, win 31–30***

***playoff game

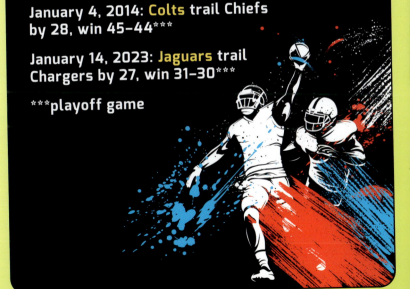

BACK AND FORTH

The Chiefs and Bills faced off in an epic playoff game on January 23, 2022. In the final two minutes, the lead changed hands four times.

2:00
Chiefs lead 26-21.

1:54
Bills lead 29-26 after a 27-yard touchdown pass from Josh Allen to Gabe Davis.

1:02
Chiefs lead 33-29 after a 64-yard touchdown pass from Patrick Mahomes to Tyreek Hill.

0:13
Bills lead 36-33 after a 19-yard touchdown pass from Allen to Davis.

0:00
Chiefs tie the game at 36 on Harrison Butker's 49-yard field goal.

The Chiefs got the last laugh. They received the overtime kickoff and marched 75 yards in eight plays. Travis Kelce caught an 8-yard touchdown pass to give Kansas City a 42-36 win.

» Kansas City Chiefs tight end Travis Kelce catches the game-winning pass in overtime to win the playoff game against the Bills in 2022.

A SNOWY FIELD-GOAL FINISH

Patriots kicker Adam Vinatieri made two clutch field goals in the same game during a snowstorm. On January 19, 2002, the Patriots hosted the Raiders in the AFC playoffs. In the final minute, Vinatieri blasted a 45-yard field goal to tie the game. Then he hit a 23-yarder to win it in overtime.

Longest NFL Game

On December 25, 1971, the Chiefs hosted the Dolphins in the AFC playoffs for the longest game in NFL history. The game went into double overtime. The game lasted 82 minutes, 40 seconds. Miami won with a 37-yard field goal.

NFL'S HIGHEST-SCORING GAMES

1966	Washington 72, New York Giants 41
2004	Cincinnati Bengals 58, Cleveland Browns 48
2018	Los Angeles Rams 54, Kansas City Chiefs 51
(tie) 2015	New Orleans Saints 52, New York Giants 49
(tie) 1963	Oakland Raiders 52, Houston Oilers 49

» Brandin Cooks scores a touchdown for the Saints during their 2015 face-off with the Giants.

Standout Plays

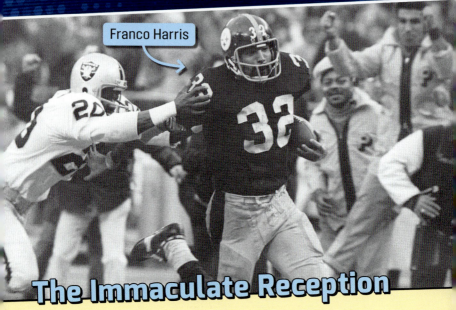

Franco Harris

The Immaculate Reception

The Immaculate Reception was a play so special it earned its own name. The Steelers hosted the Raiders in the 1972 AFC Playoffs. Pittsburgh trailed 7–6 with 22 seconds left. It was the fourth down. Steelers quarterback Terry Bradshaw threw a desperate pass over the middle of the field. Raiders safety Jack Tatum crashed into Pittsburgh's John Fuqua as the pass arrived. The ball bounced, and before it could hit the ground, Pittsburgh running back Franco Harris scooped it up. Harris ran 42 yards for the game-winning touchdown.

LONGEST FIELD GOALS

Tom Dempsey of the **Saints** was the first kicker to make a field goal of 60 yards or more. He booted a **game-winning 63-yarder** to give New Orleans a victory over Detroit in **1970**.

As of 2025, eight NFL kickers have matched or surpassed Dempsey's big kick. Here are the top three:

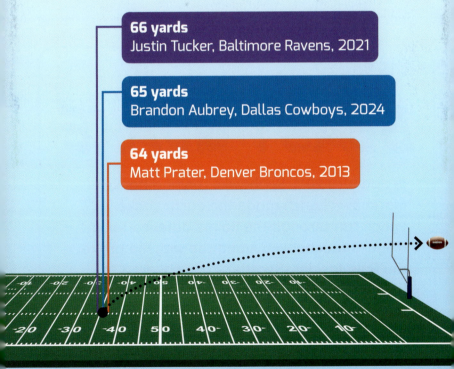

66 yards
Justin Tucker, Baltimore Ravens, 2021

65 yards
Brandon Aubrey, Dallas Cowboys, 2024

64 yards
Matt Prater, Denver Broncos, 2013

Marshawn Lynch
BEAST QUAKE

In January 2011, Seahawks running back Marshawn Lynch made the earth shake. Lynch ran through the Saints defense for a 67-yard touchdown. Along the way, he broke multiple tackles. Seattle's fans cheered so loud, it activated earthquake sensors near the stadium!

Path of the BEAST QUAKE

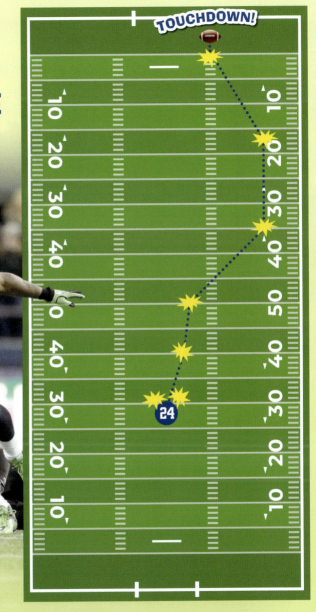

24 = Marshawn Lynch   ✸ = broken tackles

The Minneapolis Miracle

The Vikings trailed the Saints 24–23 with just 10 seconds left in their playoff game in January 2018. Minnesota had the ball at its own 39-yard line. Quarterback Case Keenum took the snap. He looked for an open receiver. Then he threw the ball toward teammate Stefon Diggs.

Diggs leapt high and made the catch at the New Orleans 34-yard line. He could have gone out of bounds so the Vikings could then try a long field goal to win it. But the Saints defensive backs whiffed on the tackle. Diggs kept his balance and sprinted the rest of the way for a touchdown!

BIGGEST RUSHING TOUCHDOWNS

In football, the longest possible play from the line of scrimmage is 99 yards. Over the years, quarterbacks and receivers have teamed up for 99-yard touchdown passes 14 times. But only two rushing plays have ever gone 99 yards. And only two more have gone 98 yards!

PLAYER AND TEAM	DISTANCE	OPPONENT	DATE
Tony Dorsett Cowboys	99 yards	Vikings	January 3, 1983
Derrick Henry Titans	99 yards	Jaguars	December 6, 2018
Ronald Jones Buccaneers	98 yards	Panthers	November 15, 2020
Ahman Green Packers	98 yards	Broncos	December 28, 2003

Team Dynasties

BRADY, BELICHICK, AND THE PATRIOTS

The New England Patriots hired Bill Belichick as head coach in 2000. That spring, they used their sixth-round draft pick on Tom Brady. Scouts thought he might be a decent backup quarterback. Nobody knew a dynasty had begun.

Belichick built the team with players he thought would work hard and play smart. Brady took over when the starting quarterback was injured early in 2001. New England won its first Super Bowl that season. From then until 2018, the Patriots had the best team in the NFL. They won a record six Super Bowls in that span.

» Bill Belichick gives Tom Brady some words of wisdom on the sideline.

NEW ENGLAND PATRIOTS SUPER BOWL HISTORY

Belichick and Brady's dynasty went to the Super Bowl nine times over 18 seasons.

- February 3, 2019: Patriots 13, Rams 3
- February 4, 2018: Eagles 41, Patriots 33
- February 5, 2017: Patriots 34, Falcons 28 (OT)
- February 1, 2015: Patriots 28, Seahawks 24
- February 5, 2012: Giants 21, Patriots 17
- February 3, 2008: Giants 17, Patriots 14
- February 6, 2005: Patriots 24, Eagles 21
- February 1, 2004: Patriots 32, Panthers 29
- February 3, 2002: Patriots 20, Rams 17

PITTSBURGH POWER

The Pittsburgh Steelers played just one playoff game their first 39 seasons. Coach Chuck Noll took over in 1969. Within three years, the Steelers had their first division title. Starting in 1974, they won four Super Bowls over the next six seasons.

The offense was led by quarterback **Terry Bradshaw**. Running back **Franco Harris** got the tough yards. Receivers **Lynn Swann** and **John Stallworth** caught touchdown passes. But the defense was their calling card. The Steel Curtain defense stopped opponents cold. The Steelers' pass rush was one of the most feared in NFL history.

Terry Bradshaw

Dynamite Drafting

In 2024, the Chicago Bears made Caleb Williams the 36th quarterback to be selected with the number one overall pick in the NFL Draft. However, being the top overall pick doesn't guarantee a successful career. Through 2024, only four of those quarterbacks have been inducted into the Pro Football Hall of Fame.

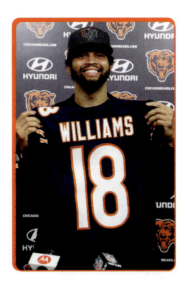

PLAYER	YEAR DRAFTED	YEAR INDUCTED INTO HALL OF FAME
Terry Bradshaw	1970	1989
John Elway	1983	2004
Troy Aikman	1989	2006
Peyton Manning	1998	2021

Kansas City Champs

Head coach Andy Reid is the winningest coach in Philadelphia (1999-2012) and Kansas City (2013-present) history. But he didn't get his first Super Bowl ring until he teamed up with Patrick Mahomes. The second-year quarterback led the Chiefs to the AFC Championship Game in 2018. They lost to Tom Brady and the Patriots. The next year, Mahomes carried the team all the way to the title. The Chiefs beat the 49ers 31-20. Kansas City went back to the Super Bowl four times over the next five years. The Chiefs brought two more Lombardi Trophies back to Kansas City.

Quarterbacks with the Most
SUPER BOWL RINGS

The key to a winning team is often a great quarterback. Only five have held the Lombardi Trophy more than twice. Brady smashed the record with the six Super Bowls he won with the Patriots. He raised the bar even higher when he led Tampa Bay to the title in 2020.

NUMBER OF RINGS	PLAYER	TEAMS
7	Tom Brady	New England Patriots Tampa Bay Buccaneers
4	Terry Bradshaw	Pittsburgh Steelers
4	Joe Montana	San Francisco 49ers
3	Troy Aikman	Dallas Cowboys
3	Patrick Mahomes	Kansas City Chiefs

LOMBARDI TROPHY
The Super Bowl champions are awarded the Lombardi Trophy. It's named for former Packers coach Vince Lombardi. His teams won the first two Super Bowls.

Close but not Quite

Twenty of the NFL's 32 teams have won the Super Bowl since it began. Twelve teams are still waiting to win. Eight have played in the big game but came away empty-handed. The **Chargers**, **Titans**, and **Cardinals** are all 0-1 in Super Bowls. The **Falcons** and **Panthers** have each lost twice, and the **Bengals** are the only 0-3 team. But the real frustration comes for fans of the **Vikings** and **Bills**. Each team has lost four Super Bowls without winning one.

» Bengals players covered in confetti after a Super Bowl loss

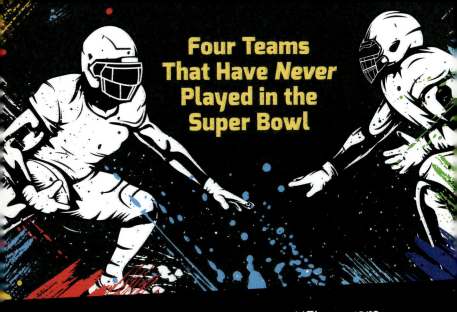

Four Teams That Have *Never* Played in the Super Bowl

- The **Browns** and **Lions** were NFL powers before the Super Bowl era.

- The **Jaguars** have come one game away from the Super Bowl three times.

- And the **Texans** are the NFL's newest franchise, so give them time.

TEAM	PRE-SUPER BOWL NFL TITLES	CONFERENCE CHAMPIONSHIP GAMES
Browns	4	0-5
Lions	4	0-2
Jaguars	not in league at that time	0-3
Texans	not in league at that time	never played

Iconic Players

Manning Brothers

Archie Manning played quarterback in the NFL for 13 seasons. But his biggest contributions to the league were two of his three sons.

Peyton Manning was the first pick of the 1998 NFL Draft.

- He led both the Colts and the Broncos to a Super Bowl title in his 17-year career.

- He also set the single season record with 55 touchdown passes in 2013.

His younger brother **Eli** was the first pick of the 2004 NFL Draft.

- He played 16 seasons with the Giants.
- Eli went 2-0 in two Super Bowls, both against Tom Brady and the Patriots.

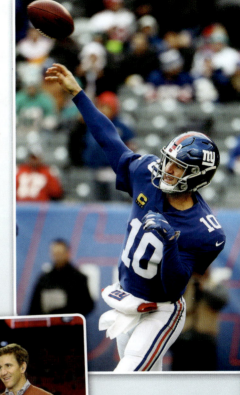

THE MANNINGCAST

Fans can catch the *ManningCast* during Monday Night Football. During the program, the Manning brothers bring on guests and break down the game together.

DOUBLE TROUBLE

Great running backs can run hard and physically punish an opponent. That's **Derrick Henry**'s style. At 6-foot-2 (188 centimeters) and 247 pounds (112 kilograms), Henry can break tackles and run over defenders. He's also fast enough to outrun the defense. Henry led the NFL in rushing yards in 2019 and 2020. In 2025, he won the AFC rushing title in his first season with the Baltimore Ravens.

Derrick Henry

Christian McCaffrey

Christian McCaffrey has a different style. He's strong and fast like Henry. But he relies on his quickness and agility to avoid tacklers. And he has great hands. McCaffrey caught 107 passes in 2018. That's more than any NFL running back has had in a season. The next year, he raised the bar with 116 catches. And he led the league with 1,459 rushing yards in 2023.

Frank Gore

NFL Career Rushing Leaders

PLAYER	YEARS PLAYED	YARDS
Emmitt Smith	1990–2004	18,355
Walter Payton	1975–1987	16,726
Frank Gore	2005–2020	16,000
Barry Sanders	1989–1998	15,269
Adrian Peterson	2007–2021	14,918

L.T.

Before Lawrence Taylor joined the Giants in 1981, linebackers were most often used to stop the run or cover receivers. The Giants had Taylor rush the passer. His speed and power made him hard to block. Taylor had more than 10 sacks in seven seasons.

» Lawrence Taylor sacks Cardinals quarterback Neil Lomax during a 1984 game.

MOST SACKS IN A SEASON

Players get credit for a sack if they tackle the quarterback behind the line of scrimmage. If two players team up for the tackle, each are credited with half of a sack. Check out the greatest pass-rushing seasons in NFL history.

NUMBER OF SACKS	PLAYER	TEAM	SEASON
23	Al Baker	Lions	1978
22.5	Michael Strahan	Giants	2001
22.5	T.J. Watt	Steelers	2021
22	Deacon Jones	Rams	1964, 1968
22	Mark Gastineau	Jets	1984
22	Jared Allen	Vikings	2011
22	Justin Houston	Chiefs	2014

»T.J. Watt sacks Ravens quarterback Lamar Jackson in a 2021 game.

JERRY RICE

Fans love to argue about who the G.O.A.T. is at different positions. But there's no argument about the best wide receiver in NFL history. That's Jerry Rice. The 49ers drafted Rice out of Mississippi Valley State in 1985. Rice wasn't the fastest runner. But he ran precise routes. He was smart. And he caught anything thrown his way.

- Rice spent 20 years in the NFL—16 with the 49ers.
- He led the NFL in receiving yards and touchdown catches in six seasons.
- He won three Super Bowls with San Francisco.
- He retired as the league's all-time leader in catches, receiving yards, and touchdowns.

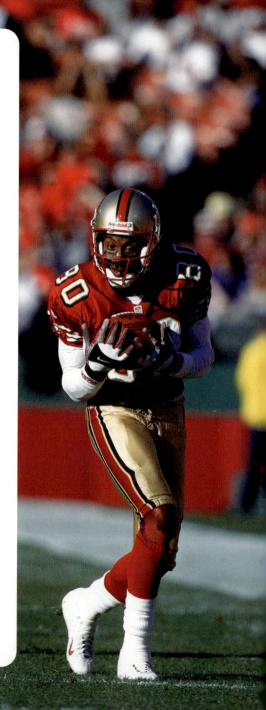

MOST CAREER TOUCHDOWNS

Players can score touchdowns many ways. They find the end zone by running the ball, catching a pass, or returning a kick or a turnover.

RUSHING
Emmitt Smith, 164
LaDainian Tomlinson, 145
Marcus Allen, 123

PUNT RETURNS
Devin Hester, 14
Eric Metcalf, 10
Brian Mitchell, 9

RECEIVING
Jerry Rice, 197
Randy Moss, 156
Terrell Owens, 153

INTERCEPTION RETURNS
Rod Woodson, 12
Darren Sharper, 11
Charles Woodson, 11

KICKOFF RETURNS
Cordarrelle Patterson, 9
Josh Cribbs, 8
Leon Washington, 8

FUMBLE RETURNS
Jason Taylor, 6
DeAngelo Hall, 5
Jessie Tuggle, 5

NON-OFFENSE
(Defense and Kick Returns)
Devin Hester, 20
Deion Sanders, 19
Rod Woodson, 17

Record Breakers

Rookie Receivers

Some young wide receivers need a few years to get used to the speed of the NFL game. But three superstars were ready on day one.

Justin Jefferson of the Minnesota Vikings made his debut in 2020. In 16 games that season, he caught 88 passes for 1,400 yards. That was more yards than any rookie wide receiver in NFL history.

Jefferson's record didn't last long. In 2021, Cincinnati Bengals rookie **Ja'Marr Chase** posted 1,455 receiving yards in 17 games.

Chase got to hold the record for two years. Then in 2024, Los Angeles Rams rookie **Puka Nacua** had 1,486 receiving yards in 17 games.

Most Rushing Yards in a Game

YARDS	PLAYER	TEAM	YEAR
296	Adrian Peterson	Vikings	2007
295	Jamal Lewis	Ravens	2003
286	Jerome Harrison	Browns	2009
278	Corey Dillon	Bengals	2000
275	Walter Payton	Bears	1977

FLIPPER'S FEAT

Rams wide receiver Willie "Flipper" Anderson set the NFL record for receiving yards in a game at New Orleans on November 26, 1989. Anderson and quarterback Jim Everett hooked up 15 times for 336 yards. His 26-yard catch in overtime set up the game-winning field goal as the Rams defeated the Saints 20–17.

Most Receiving Yards
in a Game Since 2022

YARDS	PLAYER	TEAM	YEAR
265	Amari Cooper	Cleveland Browns	2023
264	Ja'Marr Chase	Cincinnati Bengals	2024
235	Jerry Jeudy	Cleveland Browns	2024
230	DJ Moore	Chicago Bears	2023
227	CeeDee Lamb	Dallas Cowboys	2023
223	Justin Jefferson	Minnesota Vikings	2022

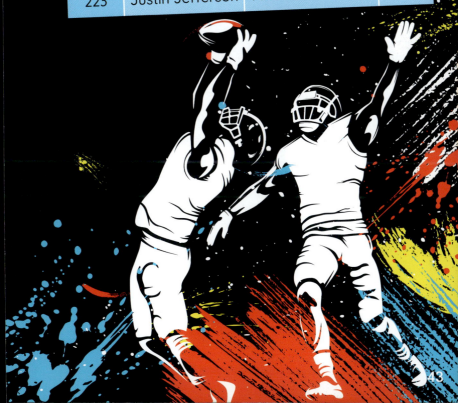

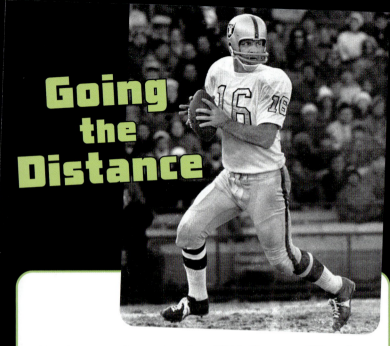

Going the Distance

By the time he retired in 1959, **George Blanda** had spent 10 years in the NFL, mostly as a backup quarterback. But the new AFL began the next year, and the league needed quarterbacks. Blanda became the Houston Oilers' starting quarterback for the next seven years. He also served as their kicker. In 1967, Blanda joined the Oakland Raiders as their kicker and backup quarterback. When he finally retired in 1975, he was 48 and had spent 26 seasons in the NFL and AFL.

By contrast, in 2023, Tom Brady retired at 45 after 23 years in the league. In 2024, Aaron Rodgers was the oldest player in the NFL at 41 years old with a 20-year career.

109-YARD PLAYS

The longest NFL play possible is 109 yards. That happens when a player starts with the ball in the back of his end zone and returns it all the way for a touchdown. It's happened three times in NFL history.

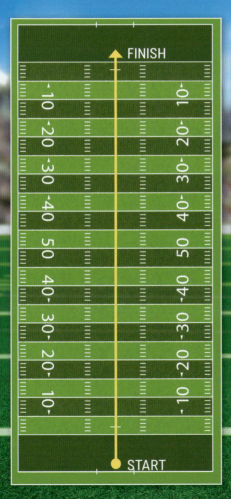

November 4, 2007 **Antonio Cromartie** of the Chargers returned a Vikings missed field goal 109 yards.

October 27, 2013 Minnesota's **Cordarrelle Patterson** took a kickoff back 109 yards against the Packers.

September 26, 2021 **Jamal Agnew** of the Jaguars returned a missed field goal against the Cardinals 109 yards.

Can't Block Derrick Thomas

Six NFL players have recorded six quarterback sacks in one game. But no one has ever had a day like Derrick Thomas had in 1990. The Kansas City linebacker led the NFL with 20 sacks that year. He got more than a third of them in one game. Thomas sacked Seattle quarterback Dave Krieg seven times on November 11, 1990. But Krieg got the last laugh. He threw a fourth-quarter touchdown pass to give the Seahawks a 17–16 win.

MOST CAREER INTERCEPTIONS

Paul Krause played safety for Washington and Minnesota from 1964 to 1979. He made 81 interceptions along the way. This record will probably never be broken. Quarterbacks have gotten much more accurate since those days. Interceptions are much harder to come by.

NUMBER OF INTERCEPTIONS	PLAYER	YEARS PLAYED
81	Paul Krause	1964–1979
79	Emlen Tunnell	1948–1961
71	Rod Woodson	1987–2003
68	Dick "Night Train" Lane	1952–65

»As of August 2025, Minnesota Vikings' Harrison Smith had the most career interceptions of any active player with 37.

About the Author

Patrick Donnelly is a sportswriter and author who lives in Minneapolis, Minnesota. He's written more than 100 books about sports. He also frequently covers Minnesota sports teams for the Associated Press.

More in This Series

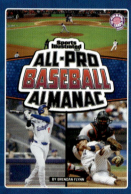
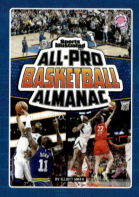
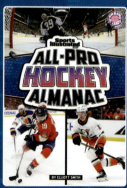
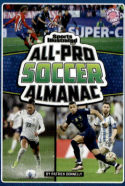